MoRe thaN WoRds

"In this beautiful book, Hannah Dunnett offers a marvellous insight into her unique creative process. She has a wonderful ability to visualise the symbolism of scripture in a way that makes it tangible and accessible; inscribing God's word onto landscapes, seascapes and everyday environments with her poetic brushstrokes and creating deeply meditative images that help us to internalise His truths. More than Words will be a much loved companion for many on their journey with Christ."

Kate Nicholas, author of *Sea Changed*, journalist and preacher

"More than Words *is more than just a beautiful book, it is also an invitation to turn down the volume on the constant noise, and to slowly soak up scripture through these uplifting pictures and their accompanying meditations. This is the perfect gift for others, but also something special for us to quietly savour ourselves."*

Cathy Madavan, writer, speaker, member of Spring Harvest Planning Group and author of *Digging for Diamonds*

MoRe than WoRds

Hannah Dunnett

MONARCH
BOOKS

Published by Monarch Books
an imprint of
SPCK Group
Studio 101, The Record Hall
EC1N 7RJ London, England

ISBN 978 0 85721 793 6

First edition 2017

Acknowledgments
Scripture quotations taken from the Holy Bible, New International Version Anglicised. Copyright
© 1979, 1984, 2011 Biblica, formerly International Bible Society. Used by permission of Hodder
& Stoughton Ltd, an Hachette UK company. All rights reserved. "NIV" is a registered trademark
of Biblica. UK trademark number 1448790.

Page 42, Proverbs 3:18 is taken from the Contemporary English Version New Testament ©
1991, 1992, 1995 by American Bible Society, Used with permission.

A catalogue record for this book is available from the British Library

Printed in September 2024

Contents

Introduction

When I was growing up, artwork and creativity were a backdrop to family life. Watercolours, oils, etchings, and tapestries hung on the walls, whilst pots, plates, vases, and model boats sat on our window sills. Alongside these were crossword puzzles, poetry books, medical journals, and prosthetic joints! Most memorably, perched on my father's bookcase was part of a skull within which you could see the tiny bones of the inner ear. Both my parents were doctors but greatly enjoyed drawing and painting as well as carpentry, gardening, and making magnificent cakes. I emerged out of a blend of creativity and a desire to understand the nuts and bolts of life.

I sketched and drew and painted with a passion as a child and art was my great love in school. For a while I thought about being an illustrator or graphic designer but then had a change of heart and decided I wanted to become a doctor like my parents. I went to Medical School and then trained as a family doctor. This was an amazing opportunity and a steep learning curve. I learned a lot about medicine, but also a lot about people, life, and myself. It challenged my character and my faith. It didn't, however, allow much opportunity for creativity, and although I loved people and was interested in science, it wasn't my passion. I wrestled with the choice I had made for several years to come.

In 2007 the church my husband Ben and I attended in Worcester held an arts week. As well as live performances, there was an exhibition of paintings, photography, and poetry. The theme was "Creator God" and I was asked to paint two large pictures to display. I began to think about how to use an image to draw someone's attention, but at the same time engage them in thinking about faith and God. It occurred to me that to paint scripture into the texture of a painting would work on two levels. It would give a deeper meaning to the painting but also illustrate and bring imagery to the words. During the exhibition I was surprised and delighted by how many people commented on them and found them inspiring.

In 2011 I finally decided to leave my job as a doctor. I began to paint more pictures and start to look for ways to exhibit them and sell them in Christian bookshops and other outlets. I exhibited at the New Wine art gallery and later at Worcester Cathedral. I began to receive emails and feedback from shops and individuals, which really motivated and inspired me to keep painting new and different pieces.

I often draw or paint from my imagination, pulling from the memories and images that have stayed with me through life. These are mostly from places I have lived or where I have spent holidays – notably the villages and countryside of Yorkshire, Worcestershire, and the Lake District. Many of these influences are found in this book, along with the scriptures and other texts that I love or have sought out.

God speaks so powerfully to people through the words in the Bible. My desire is that these pictures make scripture accessible in a fresh way. For many of us it can be hard to always pull to mind a verse or find the right passage for a certain situation, and I hope that some of the scriptures collected in these paintings provide new insight. This book can be used for personal meditation and reflection, but can also provide the basis for a discussion or small group.

And I pray that you, being rooted and established in love, may have power, together with all the the Lord's holy people, to grasp how wide and long and high and deep is the love of Christ, and to know this love that surpasses knowledge – that you may be filled to the measure of all the fullness of God (Ephesians 3:17–19).

Hannah Dunnett

The Wondrous Cross

Light of the World

Jesus refers to himself in John's Gospel as the "light of the world" (John 9:5). The purpose of the lighthouse is to guide to safety and to save from peril. This has made it a popular and much-used symbol of our salvation in Christ.

The first lighthouses were crude affairs: simple fires lit on prominences on the coast to guide ships to harbour. They evolved over time to become physical towers housing a light. Some mark the entrance to harbours, but most have been built to warn ships away from dangerous rocks or reefs.

I wanted to paint a picture on the theme of being saved, so I based the design around a lighthouse and a stormy sea. I intended the sea to be rough. I painted some of these great verses about our salvation in Christ in the waves to illustrate our need and helplessness. The lighthouse stands strong and immovable within the storm: a refuge, a beacon of light and hope. It carries the words of Jesus himself. The verses in the sky tell us not to fear, to look to God who promises to save us and help us.

~ What is your story or experience of coming to know Jesus?

~ What does it mean to you to be saved?

~ Which verses in this picture best capture your experience of salvation?

The Wondrous Cross

I have walked up several mountains in poor weather. It requires stamina and resilience to continue pushing on upwards, fighting gravity and the elements. I can remember looking up to see the path snaking on steeply ahead with still no end in sight, and that pang of desperation. However, it is a great feeling to reach the summit and see the clouds break beneath you and around you. Suddenly, great expanses of hillside that were covered by mist come into view, and what could previously only be glimpsed becomes a far-reaching view. It is these reflections and memories that underlie the inspiration for this picture.

This picture is intended to be a reflection for Easter time. I began with the words of this well-known hymn, which I have always loved. I wanted a symbol of the cross to be the focal point in the picture, and my first thought was of a wooden signpost. I liked the other meanings that could be taken from this too – for example, of Christ being "the Way". I placed a stile next to the signpost to symbolize a "crossing over" from death to life, from old to new. Beside the wall there are nettles and a thorn bush. The path leading up from the signpost is steep and winding, a tough and demanding journey to take. The sky shows the passing of a storm and the breaking light.

There are many parallels to be drawn out of this picture. I intended that some of these should be clear and others more subtle.

- ~ Which words or images in this picture have the greatest impact on you?
- ~ What other themes or parallels can you draw on from this picture?
- ~ Have you experienced a journey or physical challenge that was very demanding? How is following Jesus also a demanding and sacrificial journey?

Were the whole realm of nature mine
that were an offering far too small
Love so amazing, so divine, demands my soul, my life, my all
See from his head his hands his feet
sorrow and love
flow
mingled down
Did e'er such love and sorrow
meet
or thorns compose
so rich a crown
Forbid it Lord
that I should boast
Save in the death
of Christ my God
all the vain things
that charm me most
I sacrifice them
to his blood
When I survey the
wondrous cross
on which the
prince of
glory died
My richest gain I
count but loss and pour contempt
on all my pride

New Life

I remember asking my parents if I could be baptized. I was around seven years old and I was baptized in an outdoor swimming pool close to our church. I'm not sure how much I understood at that time, but I do know that it was the first step on a journey of faith.

I did a lot of thinking about baptism when I began this picture. I thought about the baptisms I had attended, the passages that had been read, and the songs, themes, and language used. Our experiences of baptism may be quite varied, from infant baptism and confirmation to full immersion as an adult, but we can all think about the symbolism and meaning behind the physical act.

I thought about my own experience and the baptisms described in the Bible. About the feeling of being plunged underwater, whether in a pool, a river, or the sea. Closing your eyes, holding your breath, the voices and sounds all disappearing as the water closes around your body and head. Then the noise and the light and your breath all rushing back as you resurface. The spiritual and the physical combine in a very powerful and memorable demonstration, crossing the boundaries of language and culture.

I love watching baptisms. They are such joyful and exciting occasions. To confess your faith and demonstrate it so publicly is a bold and inspiring witness. I chose verses for this picture that I hoped would capture the heart of baptism and new life, but also focus on affirmation and belonging.

~ In how many different ways is water symbolic in baptism?

~ What is your experience of baptism? What do you remember most about it?

~ Which verses in this picture speak most powerfully to you about new life?

Notes

FatheR God

Psalm 139

As a small child I got lost at Victoria Station in London. I remember the masses of people and the noise. This had been exciting and exhilarating all the time I was with my family, but when I was lost and on my own, it became terrifying and overwhelming. Fortunately, it wasn't too long before I was found by my older brother. It was such a relief to be found, to be safe.

"If I rise on the wings of the dawn, if I settle on the far side of the sea, even there your hand will guide me, your right hand will hold me fast" (verses 9–10). This was one of the first verses from the Bible that resonated with me as a child and it stuck in my mind. For God to always know where I was, and to be with me in all places, was a very comforting and reassuring truth.

This psalm is a firm favourite of mine and I took great pleasure in painting it. I wanted to represent God's presence from the highest heavens to the ocean floor. I painted the sky using twisting lines that converged in one spot. This was to try to express the enormity of God and in comparison the single identity of one person, one soul. The unfathomable truth: a God who spans the universe also knows and made the depths of our being.

~ Have you ever experienced being completely lost? How does this psalm give you reassurance?

~ How does it make you feel to be fully "known" by God?

~ Which particular words in this psalm speak to you?

Psalm 23

This psalm is incredibly well known and is used in many different circumstances. It became over-familiar to me while growing up, and it was not until a little later in life that I began to appreciate it. I was asked to lead the prayers for a friend's wedding and I wanted to find a Scripture to base them on. When I read Psalm 23 I realized it expressed so much of what I wanted to pray for my friends. A little later I painted this picture and gave it to them.

This psalm speaks of God's provision for our lives and his protection over us. It likens us to sheep, with God as our shepherd. With this central theme I felt the painting had to have as its focal point a sheep grazing beside a stream. I painted a blue sky and the sunshine to reflect gratitude and thankfulness. The water, the rich countryside, and lush grass represent the nourishment God provides for both our body and soul. The dark valley painted behind is "the valley of the shadow of death" (verse 4) that we must all face at some time. But we do so with God at our side.

This psalm is used in both times of blessing and times of difficulty. The words are powerful and speak to the heart for many. My hope is that this picture will bring fresh insight to these words for you.

~ Is this a psalm that has particular meaning for you? Why?

~ When have you experienced God's provision personally?

~ Which words echo your situation right now?

Psalm 91

My next-door neighbour asked me to paint this picture because Psalm 91 is his favourite psalm.

I have always loved mountains and hills. Whether you are looking up at them from below, or down from the summit above, they never cease to have dramatic visual impact. I'm drawn to the way the light breaks over and around them, creating shadows and contrast in colour. Having spent time walking in the English Lake District, the colours in the hills and the moody skies, along with old stone villages and farmhouses, are behind the inspiration for this picture.

I felt that the picture should illustrate a "dwelling place" and God's protection over it. The great shoulder of rock represents the ever-present and immovable hand of God upon us. The storm thunders above, but the house remains sheltered on the valley floor below. Some of the words in this psalm are very powerful and dramatic, "You will not fear the terror of night, nor the arrow that flies by day..." (verse 5), so the sheer and craggy rock face, along with the striking reds and oranges of autumn, seemed to carry them well.

Towards the end of the psalm the words become gentler and more intimate, and I have reflected this in the softer fields and the valley floor: "He will call upon me, and I will answer him; I will be with him in trouble..." (verse 15).

~ Which lines in this psalm resonate with you the most?
~ What part of the picture are you drawn to and why?
~ When have you especially felt the need for God's protection?

God is Good

There isn't a story behind this picture. It is more an expression of a theme; an attempt to pull together an image with a collection of verses that celebrate the goodness of God. It is also a call to those who feel empty to find satisfaction in meeting with God.

I wanted to express extravagant generosity, and the colours in this picture with the brightly coloured flowers and butterflies reflect this. The summer's day, the shade of the tree, and the fields full of crops all represent God's abundant provision and the beauty of his creation.

We live in a world where we are bombarded with images and messages that tell us what we need or could have in order to be satisfied. These are not necessarily bad things, but we know that they can only bring us so much. There are many verses in this picture that speak of God filling us and satisfying our spiritual hunger and thirst. The great harvest in this picture represents more than just God's provision for our physical needs. It also includes his feeding of our souls: "I have come that they may have life, and have it to the full" (John 10:10).

This picture is a reminder to myself that God loves me more than I can comprehend. His love extends beyond saving us. He desires to lavish his blessing upon us too. It is also a reminder to find my "fill" in God.

~ Which verses in this picture speak to you about God's goodness?
~ Do you find it easy to believe that God desires to bless you?
~ Where do you find yourself looking to be filled, if not from God?

Give thanks to the Lord for he is good His love endures forever

The Lord upholds all those who fall and lifts up all who are bowed down the eyes of all look to you and you give them their food at the proper time

I remain confident of this: I will see the goodness of the Lord in the Land of the Living

He has taken me to the banquet hall and his banner over me is love

I have come that they may have life and have it to the full

His divine power has given us everything we need for life and godliness through our knowledge of him who called us by his own glory and goodness

Taste and see that the Lord is good return to your rest my soul for the Lord has been good to you

And that in all things God works for the good of those who love him who have been called according to his purpose we know

What shall I return to the Lord for all his goodness to me?

He who did not spare his own son but gave him up for us all—how will he not also along with him graciously give us all things?

For he satisfies the thirsty and fills the hungry with good things

Listen, listen to me and eat what is good and your soul will delight in the richest of fare

Because of the Lord's great love we are not consumed for his compassions never fail they are new every morning great is your faithfulness

In your name I will hope for your name is good

For the Lord is good and his love endures forever his faithfulness continues through all generations

Great Delight

I painted this picture for a little girl's dedication. It is centred around a verse from Zephaniah: "The Lord your God is with you, he is mighty to save. He will take great delight in you..." (3:17).

My hope was that it would be hung on the child's bedroom or nursery wall and be read and looked at often, which is why it is so bright, vibrant, and joyful. The flowers and butterflies speak of beauty and extravagance, and capture the celebration of a new life and the delight of a parent in their child.

However, it also reminds me of a friend I spent time praying with. For her, believing that God delighted in her, that he even rejoiced over her, was a real struggle. When your life has been full of rejection it can be a long journey to recovery. So this is also a picture that speaks truth into the hearts of those who do not feel special or delighted in. It is a message of healing and restoration.

~ How does it make you feel to know that God delights in you?

~ What images or words help you to remember that God is with you?

~ Are there any current areas in your life where you need to hold on to the verses in this picture?

Wisdom

We now know such an incredible amount about the world in which we live. We are accomplishing more than we have ever done, and the advances in technology, even in my lifetime, have been staggering. However, finding meaning for life remains a constant quest for mankind, and a hidden and ellusive truth for many. The passage from Job that inspired this picture is about that search for meaning: "But where can wisdom be found? Where does understanding dwell?... God understands the way to it and he alone knows where it dwells..." (28:12, 23).

It is good to remember that when we are buried in our studies, or working hard towards a goal, the deeper meaning of life is not found in these things, however smart, motivated, or equipped we are. I chose the verse from 1 Corinthians to reiterate this: "But God chose the foolish things of the world to shame the wise..." (1:27).

The other thread running through this picture is the gift of God's word. It has power to enlighten and transform, to guide, and to comfort. Its truth cuts cleanly into our thinking and living. Those living and active words were what first inspired me to paint pictures in this way.

I hope this picture brings us to reflect on the value of wisdom and knowledge alongside the very precious gift of faith in God and how we come to find him.

~ What stories or experiences have you encountered where God has used the foolish or weak things of this world to shame the wise or strong?

~ How do we find the wisdom Job refers to?

~ When has God very clearly spoken to you through reading his word? How is it a living and active influence on your life?

Notes

Teach Me Your Ways

"Dear Lord and Father"

This is a hymn we sang many times in school assembly. I liked it then and I still do. I found it reassuring, and it gave me focus. There was little to find in my school to encourage or inspire faith. This hymn, and a few other hymns we sang, became a little window of opportunity to meet with God.

When I hear this hymn I picture the sea and fishing boats, prompted by the verse about the disciples responding to Jesus' call. I now live in Cornwall, and there are fishing boats all around me. Visually they are very appealing and have great charm, so they worked perfectly for this picture. I painted them anchored in a bay, as this hymn has a calming and peaceful effect. The words call us away from busyness and the general clamour of life and all its demands. They encourage us to seek time and space; to find a place where we can hear the voice of God and be refreshed.

For me the hymn can be said as a prayer. It is a reflection on ourselves and our constant need to realign our minds and thoughts. It is a call to find the will of God in our lives and to follow in his ways.

~ What images or memories does this hymn hold for you?

~ Do you long for stillness and peace?

~ How do you find an opportunity in your day for time to reflect or think?

dear Lord and father of mankind
forgive our foolish ways
Reclothe us in our Rightful MIND
IN purer Lives thy service find
IN deeper Reverence Praise
IN SIMPLE trust like theirs who heard
beside the Syrian sea
the gracious calling of the Lord
Let us like them without a Word
Rise up and follow thee
O Sabbath Rest by Galilee
O calm of hills above
Where Jesus knelt to share with thee
the silence of eternity
interpreted by Love
Drop thy still dews of quietness
till all our strivings cease
take from our souls the strain and stress
and let our ordered lives confess
the beauty of thy Peace
Breathe through the heats of our desire
thy coolness and thy balm
let sense be dumb
let flesh retire
Speak through the earthquake wind and fire
O still small voice of calm

Times and Seasons

I painted this picture for the front of a calendar. I wanted to illustrate the four seasons and give a sense of the rhythm to the year ahead. I also wanted to capture the ebb and flow of life.

We talk about different seasons of life with regard to age but also with regard to our experiences. There are times of great challenge and hard work, and there are times of great celebration and reward. There are times of stability and times of change. We also recognize that at some point loss is inevitable for all of us.

These seasons of life are echoed by the seasons of the natural world. Spring speaks of new life, a fresh start, of growth and nurturing: "See, I am doing a new thing!" (Isaiah 43:19). Summer is about enjoying the warmth of the sun and the rewards of the harvest: "Taste and see that the Lord is good" (Psalm 34:8). Autumn sees things coming to an end and the sowing of seeds for a future harvest: "The grass withers and the flowers fall..." (Isaiah 40:7). Winter is a cold and barren time. Here we must trust and wait; we must find faith for what we do not see or feel: "Trust in him at all times, you people; pour out your hearts to him, for God is our refuge" (Psalm 62:8).

I can look back over my life and see clearly some of the seasons I have experienced. I particularly remember the difficult ones. I didn't appreciate them at the time, but they have certainly changed me and those are the ones that have taught me the most.

~ What examples of the seasons of life do you see echoed in the natural world?

~ Looking back at the seasons you have experienced in life so far, where and when have you learned the most about God and grown the most in your faith?

~ What season do you feel you are in presently?

See I am doing a New thing
Now it Springs up
do you Not perceive it?
I am making a way in the wilderness
and streams in the wasteland
I have come that they may have life and have it to the full
For the Lord is good
and his love endures forever
Taste and see that the Lord is good
I am the alpha and the omega
he changes times and seasons
I am the first and the last
The grass withers and the flowers fall but the word of our God endures forever
Trust in him at all times you people
pour out your hearts to him
for God is our refuge
My times are in your hands
For God so loved the world that he gave his one and only son
that whoever believes in him will not perish
but have eternal life

Psalm 103

This is another favourite psalm of mine. One of my friends here in Cornwall inspired me to paint it. She read it out one evening in her home, where we had met to pray. Sometimes we hear a verse or passage that is so familiar to us, but in that time and place it makes a fresh impact on us. It's as if we are hearing it for the first time. I left that evening with an idea of how I wanted to paint this psalm.

I love the opening words. There's a call to remember and celebrate God's goodness and all he has done for us. I am also drawn to the poetry and words and expressions used. I wanted to keep the flow of the psalm in this painting and allow the eye to be drawn downwards with the words. It starts with a declaration of praise within the sky, which is painted blue and scattered with butterflies. We are then led through fields, green trees, and colourful flowers as the words speak of God's compassion, generosity, and mercy.

The most well-known verse from this psalm is painted across the centre, spanning from one side to the other: "For as high as the heavens are above the earth, so great is his love for those who fear him; as far as the east is from the west, so far has he removed our transgressions from us" (verses 11–12).

The colours change to browns at the bottom of the picture as the psalm talks of the "dust" from which we are made and the passing of generations.

This psalm inspires me, and I hope the picture encourages you to read it and be inspired by it too.

~ Is there a verse or passage in the Bible that you have discovered afresh recently?

~ How many reasons can you find in this psalm to praise God?

~ How does the flow of this image help you in your understanding of this psalm?

Proverbs 3

As parents, my husband and I hope to pass on to our children some of the things life has taught us. I am very grateful to my own parents for the many things they have helped me understand, and the wisdom they have shared with me. There have been many moments in life when I have remembered their words.

In this Bible passage, Solomon shares his wisdom as a father to his child. It is a favourite of mine, because there is such warmth and intimacy within it. I also love its poetry and the metaphors used. I read it at the wedding of some good friends just four weeks after my first child was born, so it holds memories for me, both of my friends and of becoming a parent. The verses that have stayed with me from this passage are: "Let love and faithfulness never leave you; bind them around your neck, write them on the tablet of your heart" and "Trust in the Lord with all your heart and lean not on your own understanding" (verses 3 and 5).

Solomon likens wisdom to a tree: "She is a tree of life to those who embrace her" (verse 18). This gave me the idea of painting the words of this passage into a tree. Because it's a tree of life I have added flowers, butterflies, and a stream with fish.

- ~ Are there any words of wisdom that have remained with you through your life?
- ~ Who are the people that have most influenced your life and faith in God?
- ~ Which verses from this passage have the most meaning for you?

by understanding he set the heavens in place

by his knowledge the deeps were divided

and the clouds let drop the dew

by understanding he set the heavens in place

Faithfulness Never Leave you

you prosperity and bring

Let love and

write them on the tablet of your heart

Bind them around your Neck

win favour and a good Name in the sight of god and man

Trust in the lord with all your heart

and lean not on your own understanding

In all your ways acknowledge him and he will make your paths straight

Do not be wise in your own eyes

fear the lord and shun evil

This will bring health to your body

and nourishment to your bones

My Child do Not forget my teaching but keep my commands in your heart

for they will prolong your life many years and bring

By wisdom the lord laid the earth's foundations

Blessed is the Man who finds wisdom the man who gains understanding for she is more profitable than silver and yields better returns than gold

She is more precious than rubies; nothing you can compare with her

Long life is in her right hand in her left hand are riches and honour

Her ways are pleasant ways

and all her paths are peace

She is a tree of life to those who embrace her

those who lay hold of her will be blessed

Honour the lord with your wealth with the first fruits of all your crops then your barns will be filled to overflowing

and your vats will brim over with New wine

desire

"OuR FatheR"

This is another painting inspired by a request. A primary school teacher asked me if I would create a picture based around the Lord's Prayer, but with more contemporary wording. Having two children of my own in primary school, this captured my imagination, so I wrote a poem and worked the words into this picture.

Our heavenly Father, God above, full of truth and grace and love,
Thank you that you're always there, that you hear and that you care
About the big things and the small, that fill our lives. We bring it all.
Let your words help us to know which way to turn, which way to go,
Bringing to this earthly place, a little more of heaven's grace.

Give us what we need today, to eat, to work, to love and play.
Please forgive us when we make a wrong, by aim or by mistake,
And knowing that you always do, may we forgive each other too.
This world around us is so full of different things to push and pull
Our hearts and minds in every way. Help us with this, Lord, we pray
To choose the healthy and the right, to bring your blessing and your light.

As this prayer is a model for our day-to-day prayer life, and covers our home, our sleep, our work, and our travel, I wanted the picture to have an everyday feel. I painted a typically British cloudy day! I used a semi-detached house to illustrate our differences with each other and the challenge of living in community. There are also little details added and things to spot to make this a fun and interactive picture for children.

~ When do you find it easy to pray?
~ Do you have a pattern to your praying?
~ How do you find the Lord's Prayer a helpful model?

Psalm 121

For me, walking in hills or mountains is about more than just physical exercise. It is a chance to be away from "normal life". The usual day-to-day hassles and demands are left behind, far below. The quietness and space give me time to think and reflect. Creation – be it a mountain, a lakeside, or a beach – speaks of God; it declares his praise. And in these places I find myself drawn to him.

My favourite part of this psalm is the opening: "I lift up my eyes to the hills – where does my help come from? My help comes from the Lord, the Maker of heaven and earth" (verses 1–2). I relate to the pull of the natural world (in this case the hills) and, alongside this, a searching and longing for God.

The land, the village, and the farm in this picture are imaginary, but drawn from my memories of the Yorkshire dales. The hills are rolling and gentle, with the villages tucked into the valleys below. I love the patchwork of fields and the old stone walls. The farm buildings are naturally isolated, away from community and surrounded by their land. This psalm speaks of God's protection, his watching over us, so it seemed fitting to choose a farm to be the focus. The house itself is a symbol of our protection, but there are also walls, the gate, and the dog. The words about our "coming and going" are written over the doorway. The large tree is the "shade at your right hand" (verse 5).

~ Is there a place you choose to go to when you want to be able to hear more clearly from God?

~ Which part of this psalm do you like and why?

~ We do experience tragedy and Christians are widely persecuted. How do we understand this psalm in light of this?

I lift up my eyes to the hills

where does my help come from?

My help comes from the Lord,

the Maker of heaven and earth

He will not let your foot slip

he who watches over you will not slumber

Indeed he who watches over Israel will neither slumber nor sleep

The Lord watches over you

The Lord is your shade at your right hand

The sun will not harm you by day nor the moon by night

The Lord will keep you from all harm

He will watch over your life

The Lord will watch over your coming and going

both now and for evermore

Seasoned with Salt

The kitchen is often referred to as "the heart of the home", because it is where life happens. I grew up as one of five children in quite a large house and yet, despite its many rooms, we always seemed to end up in the kitchen.

It was where my mum was usually to be found, baking, preparing a meal, or cleaning up from the last one. It was where the phone rang, the music played, and the radio jabbered. Most importantly, it was where a cup of tea was on the go along with toast and flapjacks. It was the social hub of the house, where everything from politics to semi-skimmed milk was debated, where I struggled with my maths homework, fought with my brothers, and stayed up late chatting with friends.

Other boring, but essential, tasks have to be carried out in the kitchen: washing pans, clearing up from meals, packing away shopping, sweeping the floor, sorting the rubbish. Our daily life usually begins and ends in the kitchen, from making a cup of tea and thinking about the day ahead, to putting on the dishwasher in the evening and reflecting on our triumphs or failures.

I chose earthy, gritty verses for this picture. I encourage you to look at them often to challenge the way you think and speak in the context of your relationships.

~ What memories does the kitchen you have now or the one you grew up in hold?

~ How do the commands in this picture translate into how you live every day?

~ How do these verses help challenge you on how you think about the different relationships you have?

Do Not Worry

I worked for ten years as a doctor. One of the subjects that was covered in my training, and was then ongoing in my work, was coping with uncertainty. Both patients and medical professionals face uncertainty. Not knowing, not being able to know, not having control, was one of the most challenging parts of the job, and one of the hardest things to cope with as a patient.

There are many factors within everyday life that can lead us to worry: fears, uncertainty, the weight of expectation or responsibility, and a lack of control. Whether rational or irrational, the feeling or cycle of feelings can be hard to escape. It feels like a heavy load that we cannot put down. We feel exhausted and broken by carrying it. I have felt this way. I would say that we are very fortunate as humans if we cannot recall having felt this way at some point in our lives.

The Bible speaks clearly and directly to us about worry and anxiety. I have included in this picture a collection of different verses: the words of Jesus in the Gospels, and some other passages. I have read them many times and found them so helpful. I wanted to paint a positive and uplifting picture, and the verses where Jesus draws our attention to the birds of the air and the flowers of the fields brought this image to mind.

~ Do you have a tendency towards worry and anxiety?

~ How does reflecting on Jesus' words about the birds and the flowers give you reassurance?

~ What does having the "peace of God, which transcends all understanding" mean to you?

Trust in God

My dad has always been a keen sailor. Some of my fondest childhood memories involve dinghy sailing with him. I painted this picture with him in mind.

It is about trusting God amid the uncertainty of life – not an easy thing to do. The themes of trust and faith fit well with the imagery. The sea and the sky in this picture are our ever-changing circumstances, and the boat represents ourselves as we journey through them.

We now have the privilege of living close to the sea in Cornwall. The enormity and the power of the ocean are impressed upon me more than ever. Standing on the cliff paths and looking down at the sea swelling and the waves crashing, it is easy to feel overwhelmed by its sheer force. Near the harbour, there is an old church with a wooden plaque. Carved into it is one of the verses I have used in this picture: "Mightier than the thunder of the great waters, mightier than the breakers of the sea – the Lord on high is mighty" (Psalm 93:4). This context has given the words fresh meaning to me.

When painting this picture I chose verses that have been helpful to me when I felt unsure or uncertain about life and needed to trust God. I can now see that there are several themes running through them: God's promise to be with us, faith, hope, and prayer.

I hope this picture speaks of a God who is close and ever present, even in the most difficult or challenging of times. It is a call to trust him, to cling to his words, and to have faith beyond what we can see.

~ What elements of this picture resonate with you the most?

~ How do these verses challenge you in your life right now?

~ How much do we allow or ask God to steer our path?

May the God of hope fill you with all joy and peace as you trust in Him

Why are you so downcast, o My Soul? Why so disturbed within me? Put your hope in God, for I will yet praise Him My Saviour and My God

God is our Refuge and Strength an ever present help in trouble

We hope for and certain of what we do not see

Shame you with to the very end of the Age and surely wherever you go

Now faith is being sure of what

Let us hold unswervingly to the hope we profess for he who promised is faithful

I will never leave you nor forsake you

Do not be terrified Have I not commanded you? Do not be discouraged Be strong Mightier than the thunder of the great waters Mightier than the breakers of the sea The Lord on high is Mighty

Teach me your way o Lord, lead me in a straight path

For the Lord your God will be with you

wherever you go

When you pass through the waters I will be with you and when you pass through the rivers they will not sweep over you

But take heart I have overcome the world

In this world you will have trouble

When you stand he has rescued

Blessed is the man who perseveres under trial because he will receive the crown of life that God has promised to those who love Him

Do not let your hearts be troubled Trust in God trust also in Me

Do not be anxious about anything, but in everything, by prayer and petition with thanksgiving present your requests to God, and the peace of God which transcends all understanding will guard your hearts and minds in Christ Jesus

Notes

Let Your Light Shine

By My Spirit

After I finished school at eighteen I spent six months in Brazil working with children. A song we learned and sang had this verse from Zechariah as its chorus: "'Not by might nor by power, but by my Spirit,' says the Lord" (4:6). This is a verse I have never forgotten, because the time I spent in Brazil made such an impression on me as a person and on my faith. I included the words in this picture, which is about the power of the Holy Spirit.

In John's Gospel Jesus likens the Holy Spirit to the wind, and in Acts the Holy Spirit manifests as wind and fire. This is why I chose to paint a windmill. As the wind drives the sails of a windmill to power its machinery, we are empowered by God's Spirit, bringing us to life and enabling us to do his work.

Another verse that I have included in this picture is from 2 Corinthians: "But we have this treasure in jars of clay to show that this all-surpassing power is from God and not from us" (4:7). I like the thought of us as simple vessels that contain this beautiful and unfathomable treasure, so I chose to paint it on the bricks of the windmill. The windmill in this picture sits alongside a waterway in the Norfolk Broads. This naturally gives a lovely reflection in the water, but also provides a link to John's words about baptism in the Holy Spirit.

- ~ How do you picture the Holy Spirit?
- ~ When have you been aware of the Holy Spirit empowering you?
- ~ How often are you aware of the treasure God has placed within you?

Now where the Spirit of the LORD is there is freedom

Now where the LORD is the SPIRIT

But by my Spirit, says the Lord Almighty

Not by Might Nor by Power

Be strong in the LORD and in his Mighty Power

But we have this treasure in jars of clay to show that this all surpassing power is from God and not from us

FOR GOD did not give us a spirit of timidity

I baptise you with water but he will baptise you with the holy Spirit

but a spirit of love of power and of self discipline

I PRAY also that the eyes of your heart may be enlightened in order that you may know the hope to which he has called you, the riches of his glorious inheritance in the saints and his incomparably great power for us who believe

That power is like the working

of his Mighty strength

which he exerted in Christ

when he

raised him

from the Dead

and seated

his

Right hand

in the heavenly realms

far above

all rule

and authority

Power and Dominion

City on a Hill

The village in this picture is imaginary, but it is based on a memory of driving through the hills in northern Portugal, where I have been many times with family and friends. We drove through a winding valley and glimpsed above us a village with a church perched on a hill, with fields tumbling down the sides, terraced and farmed. The colours are meant to conjure up the feel of the Mediterranean climate and the heat of the sun.

For me, it perfectly illustrated the idea that "A city on a hill cannot be hidden..." (based on Matthew 5:14). I painted the words "Let your light shine before men" in large lettering in a sky full of light and warmth because I wanted to emphasize the heart of this message – that we should be a clear and visible witness.

Working the land is hard, and the results are often at the mercy of the climate. The fields in this picture carry the words of the Beatitudes, which tell us that we find the heart of God and his limitless grace in a place of neediness and humility.

~ Which part of this picture has the most impact on you?

~ In what ways do you think you are a visible witness?

~ How can we be more visible for Christ, both as individuals and as a church?

You are the light of the world
a city on a hill cannot be hidden
neither do people light a lamp and put it under a bowl
Instead they put it on its stand and it gives light to everyone in the house
In the same way let your light shine before men, that they may see your good deeds and praise your father in heaven
Blessed are the poor in spirit for theirs is the kingdom of heaven
blessed are the meek for they will inherit the earth
Blessed are the pure in heart for they will see God
blessed are those who hunger and thirst for righteousness for they will be filled
Blessed are those who mourn for they will be comforted
Blessed are the peacemakers for they will be called sons of God
blessed are the merciful for they will be shown mercy
Blessed are those who are persecuted because of righteousness for theirs is the kingdom of heaven

Love

"Love is patient, love is kind. It does not envy, it does not boast, it is not proud" (1 Corinthians 13:4). As you might imagine, at school I was a great "doodler"; the inside of my lever arch file was completely covered in pictures, patterns, and writing. Among other things was this verse.

Over the many times that I looked at it and read it, it was actually the "nots" (what love is not) that struck me and challenged me the most. This passage grounds us in what love is and what love isn't, and it's so humbling. Our love is such a poor reflection of the perfect love we see in Christ.

The inspiration for the picture came from the fields in Yorkshire near to where I grew up. The ploughed and mown fields provide us with the food that sustains us, and this image represents these verses, which go to the core of our faith – what it is to be loved by God and to love. I remember the exact field I was walking through when I first visualized this picture. I loved the contrast between the ordered furrows and grooves, and the field's untouched borders where all manner of wild flowers would grow freely. These contrasts in colour and pattern capture the many different expressions of love. Love can be passionate, exuberant, and extravagant, but it is also often an act of daily diligence and self-sacrifice.

My hope is that this picture will fit well anywhere: a bedroom, a kitchen, a study... It carries words to be read often, which pull us back to Christ and give us perspective.

~ When you read the "Love is..." passage, which part of it can you relate to most for your situation right now?

~ What in particular in the picture helps illustrate the idea of love to you?

~ At the moment, are there places or people where it is a challenge to love?

How great is the love the Father has lavished on us, that we should be called children of God

As the Father has loved Me, so have I loved you. Now remain in my love

As the Father has loved Me, so have I loved you. Now remain in my Love. If you obey My commands you will remain in my love, just as I have obeyed my Father's commands and remain in his love. I have told you this so that my joy may be in you and that your joy may be complete

We love because he first loved us

And now I will show you the most excellent way. If I speak in the tongues of men and of angels, but have not love, I am only a resounding gong or a clanging cymbal. If I have the gift of prophecy and can fathom all mysteries and all knowledge, and if I have the faith that can move mountains but have not love, I am nothing

If I give all I possess to the poor and surrender my body to the flames but have not love, I gain nothing

Love is patient, love is kind. It does not envy, it does not boast, it is not proud. It is not rude, it is not self-seeking, it is not easily angered, it keeps no record of wrongs. Love does not delight in evil but rejoices with the truth

It always protects, always trusts, always hopes, always perseveres. Love never fails

This is how God showed his love among us: He sent his one and only Son into the world that we might live through Him

But perfect love drives out fear

There is no fear in love. But the who fear has not been made perfect in love.

Dear friends, let us love one another, for love comes from God. Everyone who loves has been born of God and knows God. Whoever does not love does not know God because God is love

But the eyes of the Lord are on those who fear him, on those whose hope is in his unfailing love

This is Love: Not that we loved God, but that he loved us and sent his Son as an atoning sacrifice for our sins

Live at Peace

"Home" is about a lot more than just bricks and mortar. It should be a place where you can relax, where you feel you can be yourself, and where you feel safe. For many of us it is also about family and community – it is the place where we feel loved and accepted, and also where that same love can be shown to others.

We have a wealth of historical and ancient buildings in England, and I really appreciate these. I particularly love the charm of older buildings, old bricks and stonework, and the pretty windows. The house that inspired this picture was an old brick cottage on a village green close to where I used to live in Worcestershire. It seemed to have all the charm you could wish for in a little house.

However, the way our houses look, both inside and outside, can tempt us to equate contentment with what we have. We can easily make it all about the "house" and not enough about a "home".

I chose verses for this picture that pick up on several themes: God's faithfulness and abundant provision for us, how our faith is central to our homes, and our impact within the community we live in. I hope it reminds us of what is important in our homes, and challenges us to play a greater role in building community.

~ What does your house or home mean to you?

~ Do you think that people who enter your home find peace?

~ How can you build community in the place where you are now?

The Gardener

Both my grandmothers were keen gardeners, and my mother is too. Over the years I have watched a lot of weeding, pruning, and planting. I have also helped with a lot of picking (and eating!), be it plums, apples, raspberries, or beans. I appreciate the time, care, and diligence it takes to make a garden beautiful or to produce a good crop of vegetables.

We have been growing vegetables with our two boys for the last couple of years. They are just old enough to appreciate that they will take weeks and months to grow, and need watering and protecting (from the rabbits!). We recently harvested the potatoes we had grown, and the excitement was infectious. It was as if we had found buried treasure. Every potato was a prize and they were all dutifully washed and counted. Being part of the preparation, watering, and waiting was what made the final result so satisfying and such a celebration!

In the Bible, there are no end of analogies with gardening and farming, trees and plants. So much of what can be observed in nature can represent what we see in our own lives and spiritual growth. I had the theme of nurturing in my mind as I painted this picture, so I placed the verse that runs down the garden path in a central position. It encourages us to be rooted in the love of Christ.

~ What references to gardens, gardening, or farming come to your mind from the Bible?

~ Do you have examples of where your own toil and lengthy work have resulted in great reward?

~ What are you involved in growing or nurturing within your own life or the life of the church?

Restoration

I painted this picture as a final design for the collection in this book. I have wanted to paint something on this subject for some time. Restoration and healing are such powerful themes, because so many of us ache for our own healing or the healing of others. We long to see the restoration of a relationship, a community, or even a nation.

I was working on this picture the day of the terror attack in France on Bastille Day, 2016. That morning I had painted some of the words from Revelation: "He will wipe every tear from their eyes. There will be no more death or mourning or crying or pain, for the old order of things has passed away" (21:4); "And the leaves of the tree are for the healing of the nations" (22:2). These words felt so timely and poignant on that morning.

God can and does heal. He brings restoration in so many ways. Jesus' death and resurrection have bought us spiritual restoration and new life. However, we still wrestle with why some don't experience healing despite great faith, and why our prayers seemingly go unanswered. We often can't find explanations for the suffering around us, but we can look ahead to the restoration of all things that God promises will come about.

This picture is of a house being restored to its original glory. An overgrown and neglected garden is being slowly cleared and put in order. Walls are being rebuilt, windows painted and refurbished, weeds are being pulled out, and brambles cut away. There is meant to be plenty of meaning to find in this picture. The tree on the hill is symbolic of the cross; the apple tree, the garden of Eden.

I want this picture to bring hope. I trust that it speaks of a healing and restoration that has already begun and will eventually be completed.

~ How does this picture bring you fresh hope?

~ When you look at and read the verses in this picture, is there a person or a situation that comes to mind?

~ Is there a verse or part of this picture that helps you pray for their healing or for restoration?

Notes

Bible quotations within the illustrations
Quotations are taken from the NIV 1984 and NIV 2011.

Page 11: 'Fear not… you' Isaiah 43:1; 'The Lord your God… save' Zephaniah 3:17; 'My soul… my fortress… be shaken' Psalm 62:1–2; 'To you I call O Lord my rock' Psalm 28:1; 'For it is by grace… gift of God' Ephesians 2:8; 'Salvation is found… must be saved' Acts 4:12; 'heal me O Lord…shall be saved' Jeremiah 17:14; 'The Lord is my light… whom shall I fear' Psalm 27:1 (NIV 1984). 'For I am the Lord… I will help you' Isaiah 41:13; 'Our God is a God who saves' Psalm 68:20; 'He rescues and he saves' Daniel 6:27; 'I am the light… light of life' John 8:12; 'I will turn the darkness into light before them' Isaiah 42:16; 'Say to those with fearful… will come' Isaiah 35:4; 'Everyone will be saved' Joel 2:32 (NIV 2011).

Page 15: 'If anyone is in Christ… new has come' 2 Corinthians 5:17; 'Fear not for I have redeemed you… you are mine' Isaiah 43:1; 'If you confess… you will be saved' Romans 10:9 (NIV 1984). 'In him was life… mankind' John 1:4; 'he set my feet on a rock… to our God' Psalm 40:2–3; 'but you were washed, you were… of our God' 1 Corinthians 6:11; 'Cleanse me with hyssop… whiter than snow' Psalm 51:7; 'This is my son… well pleased' Matthew 3:17; Matthew 17:5; 2 Peter 1:17; 'I will not forget you… palms of my hands' Isaiah 49:15–16 (NIV 2011).

Page 21: Psalm 139:1–10, 13–18, 23–24 (NIV 1984).

Page 23: Psalm 23 (NIV 1984).

Page 25: Psalm 91:1–6, 9–16 (NIV 1984).

Page 27: 'In your name… good' Psalm 52:9; 'Listen listen… richest of fare' Isaiah 55:2; 'his divine power… goodness' 2 Peter 1:3; 'He has taken me' Song of Solomon 2:4 (NIV 1984). 'Give thanks to the Lord… endures forever' Psalm 106:1; 107:1; 118:1, 29; 136:1; 'The Lord upholds… proper time' Psalm 145:14–15; 'I remain confident… living' Psalm 27:13; 'I have come… ' John 10:10; 'Taste and see that the Lord is good' Psalm 34:8; 'Return to your rest, my soul, for the Lord has been good to you' Psalm 116:7; 'And we know that… his purpose' Romans 8:28; 'What shall I return to the Lord for all his goodness to me?' Psalm 116:12; 'He who did not spare… all things?' Romans 8:32; 'For he satisfies the thirsty… good things' Psalm 107:9; 'Because of the Lord's great love… your faithfulness' Lamentations 3:22–23; 'For the Lord is good… generations' Psalm 100:5 (NIV 2011).

Page 29: 'The Lord your God… with singing' Zephaniah 3:17 (NIV 1984). 'The Lord bless you… to you' Numbers 6:24–25; 'You hem me in… upon me' Psalm 139:5; 'I am he who will… carry you' Isaiah 46:4; 'For I know… a future' Jeremiah 29:11 (NIV 2011).

Page 31: 'For the Word… sword' Hebrews 4:12; 'But wisdom… actions' Matthew 11:19; 'The Spirit… power' Isaiah 11:2; 'Your word is a lamp… path' Psalm 119:105; 'There is a time… heaven' Ecclesiastes 3:1 (NIV 1984). 'But where… where it dwells' Job 28:12, 23; 'But God chose the… strong' 1 Corinthians 1:27; 'Choose my… with her' Proverbs 8:10–11; 'For the Lord gives… understanding' Proverbs 2:6; 'Remember your creator in the days of your youth' Ecclesiastes 12:1 (NIV 2011).

Page 39: 'See I am doing… wastelands' Isaiah 43:19; 'I have come that… full' John 10:10; 'For the Lord… forever' Psalm 100:5; 'Taste and see that the Lord is good' Psalm 34:8; 'I am the first and the last' Revelation 1:17; 'I am the Alpha and the Omega' Revelation 22:13; 'He changes times and seasons' Daniel 2:21; 'The grass… forever' Isaiah 40:8; 'Trust in him… our refuge' Psalm 62:8; 'My times are in your hands' Psalm 31:15; 'For God so loved… eternal life' John 3:16 (with adaptation of 'shall' to 'will') (NIV 2011).

Page 41: Psalm 103:1–5, 8–17 (NIV 1984).

Page 43: Proverbs 3:1–10, 13–20 (with adaptation of 'son' to 'child') (NIV 1984).

Page 45: Author's own adaptation based on Matthew 6:9–13; Luke 11:2–4.

Page 47: Psalm 121 (NIV 1984).

Page 49: 'Be devoted…above yourselves' Romans 12:10; 'Each one should… forms' 1 Peter 4:10 (NIV 1984). 'Therefore, as God's chosen… patience' Colossians 3:12; 'Above all, love each other… of sins' 1 Peter 4:8; 'And over all these virtues… unity' Colossians 3:14; 'Forgive as the Lord forgave you' Colossians 3:13; 'Love must be sincere. Hate what is evil; cling to what is good' Romans 12:9; 'Be joyful in hope… patient in affliction… faithful in prayer… practise hospitality' Romans 12:12–13; 'Never be lacking in zeal… the Lord' Romans 12:11; 'Offer hospitality to one another without grumbling' 1 Peter 4:9; 'Humble yourselves… time… Cast… for you' 1 Peter 5:6–7; 'Let your conversation… answer everyone' Colossians 4:6 (NIV 2011).

Page 51: 'Do not be anxious… minds in Christ Jesus' Philippians 4:6–7; 'See how the lilies… worry about itself' Matthew 6:28–30, 34 (NIV 1984). 'Come to me… give you rest' Matthew 11:28; 'Cast all your anxiety on him because he cares for you' 1 Peter 5:7 (NIV 2011).

Page 53: 'Why are you so downcast… my God' Psalm 42:5, 11; 43:5; 'Now faith is… do not see' Hebrews 11:1; 'Teach me… straight path' Psalm 27:11; 'Have I not commanded… will be with you… wherever you go' Joshua 1:9; 'Blessed is the man who… love him' James 1:12; 'Do not let your hearts… also in me' John 14:1; 'Do not be anxious… in Christ Jesus' Philippians 4:6–7 (NIV 1984). 'May the God… trust in him' Romans 15:13; 'God is our refuge and strength, an ever-present help in trouble' Psalm 46:1; 'I will never leave you nor forsake you' Joshua 1:5; 'Let us hold unswervingly… is faithful' Hebrews 10:23; 'and surely I am with you… the age' Matthew 28:20; 'Mightier than… high is mighty' Psalm 93:4; 'In this world… overcome the world' John 16:33; 'When you pass… over you' Isaiah 43:2 (NIV 2011).

Page 59: 'For God did not… discipline' 2 Timothy 1:7 (with amendment to order of 'love' and 'power'); 'I pray also that… who believe… That power is like… dominion' Ephesians 1:18–21 (NIV 1984). 'Not by might… almighty' Zechariah 4:6; 'Now the Lord is… freedom' 2 Corinthians 3:17; 'Be strong in the Lord and in his mighty power' Ephesians 6:10; 'But we have this treasure… not from us' 2 Corinthians 4:7; 'I baptise you with… holy Spirit' Mark 1:8 (NIV 2011).

Page 61: 'You are the light… Instead… In the same way… heaven' Matthew 5:14–16; 'Blessed are the poor… kingdom of heaven' Matthew 5:3–10 (NIV 1984).

Page 63: 'how great… children of God' 1 John 3:1; 'As the father…may be complete' John 15:9–11; 'And now I will show you… love never fails' 1 Corinthians 12:31–13:8 (NIV 1984). 'We love because he first loved us' 1 John 4:19; Dear friend, let us love…This is love… sins' 1 John 4:7–10; 'But the eyes of the Lord… unfailing love' Psalm 33:18; 'There is no fear in love. But perfect love drives out fear' 1 John 4:18 (NIV 2011).

Page 65: 'The Lord is faithful… he has made' Psalm 145:13; 'Let the light… dwell in safety' Psalm 4:6–8; 'Unless the Lord… in vain' Psalm 127:1; 'Trust in the Lord… your heart' Psalm 37:3–4; 'You have made known to me the path of life' Acts 2:28; 'Lord you have assigned… inheritance' Psalm 16:5–6 (NIV 1984). 'If it is possible… everyone' Romans 12:18; 'I am the vine you are the branches' John 15:5; 'Love you neighbour as yourself' Leviticus 19:18; Matthew 19:19; 22:39; Mark 12:31, 33; Luke 10:27; Romans 13:9; Galatians 5:14; James 2:8; 'Bless those… mourn' Romans 12:14–15; 'Live in harmony with one another' Romans 12:16; NIV 'But as for me… the Lord' Joshua 24:15 (NIV 2011).

Page 67: 'But the fruit… self-control' Galatians 5:22–23; 'you did not choose… will last' John 15:16; 'and I pray… of God' Ephesians 3:17–19; 'So neither he… things grow' 1 Corinthians 3:7 (NIV 1984). 'I am the true vine… gardener' John 15:1; 'Let my teaching… tender plants' Deuteronomy 32:2; 'Peacemakers… righteousness' James 3:18; 'those who sow in tears… joy' Psalm 126:5; 'But grow… Jesus Christ' 2 Peter 3:18 (omits 'and saviour'); 'The Lord has done… filled with joy' Psalm 126:3 (NIV 2011).

Page 69: 'Praise be to… or fade' 1 Peter 1:3–4; 'Restore us… be saved' Psalm 80:7; 'You will go out… will grow' Isaiah 55:12–13 (omitted 'tree' after 'pine'); 'I have loved… again' Jeremiah 31:3–4 (NIV 1984). 'He will wipe… has passed away' Revelation 21:4; 'For the son… the lost' Luke 19:10; 'and the leaves… nations' Revelation 22:2; 'I have heard… heal you' 2 Kings 20:5; 'See I am… perceive it?' Isaiah 43:19; 'They will rebuild… devastated' Isaiah 61:4; 'For I am the Lord who heals you' Exodus 15:26; 'Its ruin I will rebuild and I will restore it' Acts 15:16 (omits 's' from 'ruins'); 'I will turn… sorrow' Jeremiah 31:13 'Be strong… hope in the Lord' Psalm 31:24 (NIV 2011).

Hymn quotations used within the illustrations

Page 13: *When I Survey the Wondrous Cross* by Isaac Watts (1707).

Page 37: *Dear Lord and Father of Mankind* by John Greenleaf Whittier (1872).